PUBLIC LIBRARY

AUTHOR:

TITLE:

DATE: BORROWER'S NAME:

Farrar Straus Giroux Books for Young Readers • An imprint of Macmillan Publishing Group, LLC • 120 Broadway, New York, NY 10271 • Text copyright © 2021 by Lydia M. Sigwarth • Illustrations copyright © 2021 by Romina Galotta • All rights reserved • Color separations by Bright Arts • Printed in China by Toppan Leefung Printing Ltd., Dongguan City, Guangdong Province • Designed by Aram Kim • First edition, 2021 • 10 9 8 7 6 5 4   mackids.com • Library of Congress Cataloging-in-Publication Data is available. • ISBN 978-0-374-31390-6 • Our books may be purchased in bulk for promotional, educational, or business use. Please contact your local bookseller or the Macmillan Corporate and Premium Sales Department at (800) 221-7945 ext. 5442 or by email at MacmillanSpecialMarkets@macmillan.com. • The illustrations in this book were done in watercolors, colored pencils, and graphite and were assembled or touched up digitally.

Hello, reader!

I make a radio show. We do stories about all sorts of people. One of our producers, Stephanie Foo, loves libraries so much that she made a story for the radio about someone named Lydia. Lydia had a pretty life-changing experience in the library. And when we told our listeners, they went wild for it. Bananas. You get the idea. They really liked it.

Afterward, Lydia wrote her own version of the story, and that's the book you're holding in your hands.

I think I need to mention here that like Lydia and Stephanie, I am also a massive, hardcore, nonstop, colossal library fan. When I was little, on one of my regular trips to the Baltimore County Public Library, I discovered there were books that teach magic tricks. That totally blew my mind. These incredible secrets were just sitting on a shelf for anyone to learn—for absolutely free! I started performing magic shows. Like, for money. Real money! I did this for years. It taught me how to speak in front of a crowd and all sorts of other skills I use on the radio every week.

Also, I can still make a coin vanish. Here, watch this. Okay. It's gone! Humph. Maybe you didn't see that? I swear: In between writing down these words . . . I really made it disappear. If you and I meet someday, I'll do it for you in person. Till then, I hope you like Lydia's story as much as our listeners did!

Ira Glass, host and executive producer of *This American Life*

DEAR
LIBRARIAN

Lydia M. Sigwarth   Romina Galotta

Farrar Straus Giroux

New York

Dear Librarian,

May I tell you a story?

It's about me, and it's about you, and it's about my Library Home.

It happened when I was five years old.

Me and my mom and my dad and my five big sisters and one baby brother all had to leave Colorado and go to Iowa, where Grandma was.

My dad needed a new job, and we needed a new place to live.

In Iowa, I missed my little blue home with the big maple tree.

I missed my red roller skates packed away in the big truck.

I missed my sunny backyard with lots of space to run and play.

I missed my best friend, Little Becca.

But most of all, I missed having a home.

In Iowa, I didn't have a home to live in, just houses.

Five big sisters and one baby brother and a mom and a dad
are a lot of people, so we lived in a lot of different places.

Some days we lived at Aunt Linda's house.

Aunt Linda had a pretty pink bathtub for fancy bubble baths.

But Aunt Linda's house was full of nice things.

Nice things you shouldn't touch because they aren't yours.

Some days we lived at Cousin Alice's house.

Cousin Alice had her own family to take care of,

but she let us sleep in her tiny, cozy basement.

In Cousin Alice's basement, there was a big couch and bouncy mattresses.

Every night was a giant sister sleepover!

But even a snuggly sleepover was a little too crowded for all of us.

Some days we stayed at Grandma's house.

Grandma lived right by a park with swings and space to run and spin.

But there weren't any friends at Grandma's park.

Mom said it was very generous of everyone to let us live at their houses. But . . .

Grandma's house was too small,
Aunt Linda's house was too nice,
and Cousin Alice's house already
had a family.
Nowhere was home.

Nowhere had a special spot
just for me.

Then one day Mom took me and my five big sisters
and one baby brother to a new place.
   Not a house, but a big building
with stone columns and tall, tall steps.

The Library.

There was a sunny window that took up a whole wall.

There were rows and rows of books,

and baskets of toys, and a puppet theater.

There was so much to do and so much space to do it in!

At the window, I could watch people on the street.

Or I could skip down the rows of books with my brother.

Or I could make up stories with my sisters.

There was enough space at the Library for all of us.

Then I found a special spot just for me.
Up the tall stairs, across from the sunny window,
was a round desk.
It was my favorite spot because . . .

Behind that desk was my new friend.

She had kind eyes, a gentle face, and a laugh like bubbles.

That friend was the Librarian, and that Librarian was you.

LIBRARIAN

You looked me right in the eyes and listened to me like I was a grown-up.

You helped me find a book about princesses, and then you sat down on the floor to read it to me.

After that, Mom and Dad brought
me to the Library all the time.

Every day, you gave me a hug.
Every day, you made me feel
safe and happy.

Those days, the Library
was like a home.
My own special home.
(Even though it wasn't
a house.)

Later that year, my mom and dad and my five big sisters
and one baby brother all went to live in a big brown home
with a tall willow tree.

I could zoom around in my red roller skates again.

But I still visited my Library Home
to be in my favorite spot and read
books, and to be home with you,
my Library Friend.

Now, my dear Librarian, I'm a grown-up, but I still go to the Library every day.

Because I'm a Librarian, just like you.

You gave me a Library Home, so I wanted to make one, too.

For kids with little blue homes,

and big brown homes,

and no homes at all.

So I did.

Dear Reader,

This book is based on what really happened to my parents, my siblings, and me when I was a little girl. For six months, my family stayed with various loved ones while we were homeless and looking for our own place to live.

Homelessness affects around 2.5 million children every year. Many go years without experiencing a stable home life. Each child faces different challenges. Each child has their own individual story. My experience was unique to me alone.

I am now a children's librarian in Wisconsin. In 2018, with the help of the radio show *This American Life*, I reunited with the librarian I wrote about in this book, Deb Stephenson. I thanked her for inspiring me, and it was truly one of the most amazing experiences of my life. Maybe there is a librarian in your life who has inspired you, too. If so, tell them! And maybe give them some chocolate—we usually like chocolate.

If you would like to learn more about libraries and the work librarians do, please visit the American Library Association at ALA.org.

Happy Reading!

Lydia M. Sigwarth